Be More

Assertive

Stop People Pleasing, Develop Assertive Communication Skills, Learn To Set Boundaries and Be Yourself

Thomas Lee Watson

Table of Contents

Introduction

The funny thing about society is that it often talks a good game regarding certain public values. Since childhood, we have been encouraged to help others, to think of something bigger and better than ourselves. We have even been told that we should sacrifice a little bit of ourselves for some sort of greater good.

It's all about the cost. It's all about giving back. It's all about being part of the solution rather than continuing to be part of the problem. Indeed, in certain circles, we have even been pushed to become a "man for others". Selflessness has long been an enduring positive social virtue.

We could all agree that there is a lot of value to individuals working towards a common goal and setting aside selfish ambition and personal needs to achieve that united goal. But this doesn't apply across the board. It definitely doesn't apply in all circumstances to all people at all times.

While there is space for accommodation and helping others, you can not overdo it. there is a line between pitching in to help others and becoming some sort of doormat. If you think about it hard enough, you're not really doing anybody much favors when you allow yourself to be taken advantage of.

This happens quite a bit. People's kindness are often exploited. You start out trying to help somebody as a favor and before you know it, they expect you to do their bidding automatically. They expect you to respond out of obligation without thinking.

As the old saying goes, if you give an inch, they will take a mile. It's not unusual for people to be given a hand in assistance and then they expect the arm. If you've ever been on the receiving end of this, please understand that you're not doing yourself any favors.

If you want to move up in this world and if you want to achieve your hopes and dreams, you have to learn how to be more assertive. You have to assert yourself and one foundational definition of this is the ability to create boundaries.

In other words, you have to learn how to say no.

Warren Buffet's Secret To HUGE SUCCESS

No other than the legendary American investor and business leader Warren Buffet said, **"The difference between successful people and really successful people is that really successful people say no to almost everything."**

This is kind of shocking. I mean, after all, successful people succeed primarily because they are able to work with other people to achieve their goals. Have you ever noticed that successful entrepreneurs work with groups of people so that everybody achieves their goal while the entrepreneur gets a massive reward. That's how it works.

It seems that one of the most successful proponents of capitalism, Mr. Warren Buffet himself, is championing the opposite view. Generally speaking, creating wealth among people involves getting people to say yes. Here he is, talking about really successful people saying no. Not just from time to time. But saying no to "almost everything".

The Genius of Saying No

It's easy to think that when you're getting along with other people that you are getting stuff done. Well, that's an illusion. When you are bending over backwards, doing favors for anybody requesting them, you're overlooking one important factor: opportunity costs.

Last time I checked, people can not be at 2 places at once. You're either doing one thing or you're doing another. You can't be doing both. There is this common fiction of multitasking. It's very tempting. It's definitely very appealing. Who wouldn't want to do 2 things at once?

But when you look at multitasking, you're not doing 2 things at once. You're definitely not doing many things at once. What you're doing is you're working on one thing, you stop it, you do another and then you stop that and then you go back to the previous task or to a new task.

This can happen in rapid succession and you may get the misleading impression that you're actually doing many different things. No, you're not. Understanding that multitasking is a lie highlights the importance of opportunity costs.

Since you can't do 2 things at once just as you can no be at 2 places at the same time, you have have to make a choice. What if the favors that you're doing for other people delivers a big fat 0 to your life? What if you could have been doing something else for yourself or for other people which could have produced greater value?

Please understand that there are always opportunity costs involved. This is the whole point Warren Buffet is making. Mr. Buffet is so rich that theoretically speaking, it doesn't make sense for him to pick up a $20 bill on the ground.

He probably makes thousands of dollars every single minute. If you break that down, when he picks up a $20 bill that's been left on the ground, he's actually losing money. Learn to say no. It's probably going to be one of the most profitable things you would ever do in your life. How come?

It will focus your mind on opportunity costs. In other words, you can give yourself the opportunity of reorienting every single day of your life to something that actually adds a tremendous amount of value to your life.

Steve Jobs and the Power of Focus

Steve Jobs is a giant in American information technology and innovation. He embodied the American ideal of somebody coming from a very humble back ground and becoming a titan of industry. He did this because of the power of concentration.

He knew that innovation requires a tremendous amount of focus. He also knew that there are so many distractions out there. There are many tasks that may seem important enough so that they distract you from what you should be doing.

It can be very confusing. You may reach a point where you can't even tell tasks apart in terms of their ultimate value and importance. The founder of Apple computers and Next and the CEO of Pixar famously said, **"It's only by saying no that you can concentrate on what's important."**

This goes beyond opportunity costs. Warren Buffet's analysis behind saying no is definitely enlightening because it highlights the concept of opportunity costs. Steve Job's quote focuses on importance.

Something may be important, but it may not be paying off big time right now. But it can lead to tremendous innovation, disruption and growth in the future. Regardless, when you're bending over backwards trying to accommodate everybody, you are distracted from what is important. You are distracted and side tracked from doing the things that can eventually put you on top because of your tremendous focus.

He highlighted the importance of focus with the following quote in 1997 during the Apple World Wide Developers Conference. **"People think focus means saying yes to the thing you've got to focus on. But that's not what it means at all. It means saying no to the hundred other good ideas that there are. You have to pick carefully. I'm actually as proud of the things we haven't done as the things I have done. Innovation is saying no to one thousand things."**

This is crucial. The importance of focusing on what truly is important is crucial. It will be great if what determined what is "important" can be quantified in dollars and cents. But it's not that easy nor is it shallow.

As Steve Jobs said, there are tons of good ideas out there. Almost all of these have dollar figures. If you're just going to use the opportunity cost analysis similar to the line of thinking of Warren Buffet, it may not be optimal.

You have to think of the big picture. You have to know of what to focus on regardless of its comparatively low value now based on what it can possibly lead to. Remember, Steve Jobs' stock and trade was innovation and disruption.

He was able to do this not because he was just mastering stuff that people were already doing or people were focusing on. He looked beyond what they were doing. He looked at alternative paths. He looked at something higher.

You have to understand this dimension to the ability of saying no to others so you can see the full extent of the consequences of this ability you are trying to cultivate.

Chapter 1: Why Is It So Tempting to Be A People Pleaser?

It seems so pleasant. Who wouldn't want to please other people? Who wouldn't want to make other people happy? Who wouldn't want to be part of the solution instead of continuing to contribute to the problem?

But when you look deeper into people pleasing, it turns out that it's not what you thought it was. People pleasing is a process, first and foremost. It is not a single act. It is not a single description. It is a process.

Just like any other process, you have to pay close attention to motivation. Why are you doing certain things when certain stimuli are present? Why can you be counted on when certain conditions materialize?

Here's the problem with people pleasing. It is motivated primarily by a need to be validated by other people and to earn their approval. That's what you're doing it for. You're not doing it to contribute to a greater cause, per se. It is primarily personal. It's primarily done due to a need for some sort of one to one validation.

People pleasing is a continuous process. In other words, it happens on a generally consistent basis. It's not a one time kind of thing. Ultimately, it has one key determining characteristic. You are putting other people's needs ahead of your own.

We all have needs. Those needs are not going to go away. When you constantly feel the need to please other people, your default position is to put other people's needs ahead of you.

People Pleasing Is Not As Obvious As You Think

Don't be tempted into thinking that it's very easy to spot people pleasing. No it isn't. It's actually unconscious and habitual. You really have to connect the dots because there's a lot of subtlety to it. In fact in many cases, it involves manipulation. But not what you think.

You're trying to manipulate how other people perceive you by doing them favors. In other words, you're trying to bribe them. But the real victim here is you. You become so addicted to people saying you're a good person and you having a good reputation that at the end of the day, you always come out last because you're always trying to put others first.

You become dependent on their approval and this warps you. Any slight bit of disapproval or critique is enough to ruffle your feathers.

Relationship with the Psychological Condition of "Co-dependency"

Please understand that being a people pleaser doesn't mean you're automatically "co-dependent". However, there is a thin line and it's very easy to enter into co-dependency. If your number one goal in life is to please other people and, by the same token, avoid conflict with them, then you become trapped in this cycle of always trying to put other people first because you're so afraid of the negative consequences.

You don't want to let people down. You don't want people talking behind your back. You don't want to be criticized. So on and so forth. Even if you don't feel like it, even if you are making yourself miserable, even if it hurts, even if it's gotten downright uncomfortable and inconvenient for you, you still find yourself doing it.

This compulsion makes you feel stuck. It's like you're trapped. You've entered co-dependency.

How Do You Know If You're A People Pleaser?

If any 3 of these statements apply to you, there's a high chance you are a people pleaser. In the next chapter, I'm going to explain why this is a serious problem.

You take actions based primarily on what people would think of you.

You have a tough time saying no to requests made of you.

You agonize about having to say no.

You feel like you can't live without people approving of you.

Other people's opinions matter a lot to you and you spend a lot of your thoughts thinking about whether you disappointed or offended somebody.

You have a tough time sharing your opinions because you're afraid it might not be received all that well by others around you.

You hold back from sharing what you truly think because you're afraid that somebody later on might take it the wrong way.

You don't know where yourself ends and where the team begins.

You're constantly fascinated and interested in what's going on in other people's lives.

You tend to blow any kind of criticism or even neutral critique out of proportion.

The idea of rejection either makes you really sad or angry.

You don't think you are capable of much unless you team up with other people.

You feel safer in a large group of people.

You are so generous that it has become some sort of fault.

You would rather go without than having somebody you care about suffer.

You have a tough time expressing negative emotions to other people.

The worst thing that you can imagine is for people in your life to turn their back on you.

You often find yourself ending up with a raw deal because you did favors for your family, friends and associates.

Your mood is totally dependent on how other people are feeling around you.

You are an emotional sponge quickly absorbing the excitement, depression, anger or joy of your environment.

You have no problem saying what you have to say and doing what you have to do just to be liked and admired.

You will pay a very high price for the respect and admiration of others.

If somebody doesn't give you the praise you think you deserve, you interpret it as a borderline insult.

You constantly compare yourself to other people.

You always back down when caught in an argument.

You always look at the good things people have done for you in the past even if they're not being all that pleasant or good to you now.

If even 3 of the statements above apply to you, there is a good chance that you are a people pleaser. This is not a good thing. See the next chapter.

Chapter 2: 9 Reasons You Should Stop People Pleasing Immediately

People pleasing is bad news because of 9 key problems. These problems will ensure a lousy life. You're not going to live up to your fullest potential. You're not going to live life to the fullest. That's how bad people pleasing can be.

It is very corrosive and tricky. On the surface, it looks like you're very popular. On the surface, it looks like you're very well adjusted. But don't be surprised if deep down inside, you're dying. All of us have a personality. All of us are unique. But your individuality is the first thing that has to go if you are pleasing other people.

How can it flourish? You live solely for the approval of others. The more powerful, distinguished, rich, beautiful and desirable they are, the more you feel that you have to bend over backwards because the stakes are all that much higher for you.

That's not a way to live. It's as if you're living in your own personal prison and the worst part is only you would know. When people look at you, they smile, they're happy because they're getting what they want from you. Why shouldn't they smile?

But here you are. Putting yourself last. Foregoing opportunities for tremendous personal growth and essentially remaining a small, weak, vulnerable emotional child. If the foregoing discussion wasn't enough to clue you in on the problem of people pleasing, here are the 9 things that you need to focus on.

1. You Put Unnecessary Stress On Yourself

When you're busy trying to please other people, you put a tremendous amount of stress and pressure on your emotions. It's as if you're always last. It's as if you are giving and giving and giving and everybody else is taking and taking and taking.

On top of all this, you're forced to wear a smile. That's a tremendous amount of pressure. That's a total disservice to you. But the worst part to all of this is that it's all voluntary and you want it to happen.

2. You Never Get The Reward You Deserve

What do you think happens when you are trying to please everybody? What do you think happens when you can be counted on to roll over when somebody needs something done? What happens when they look at you as the "go to" girl or guy for solutions to certain problems?

Believe it or not, they don't look at you as some sort of hero. I know, it's hard to believe and accept. But that's exactly what's happening. They look at you as a patsy. They look at you as somebody they can take for granted.

Ultimately, if you keep bending over backwards to please other people, eventually, your opinions and feelings don't matter. How can they matter? Because obviously, you have no individuality of your own. Otherwise, you would've put up a fight. Otherwise, you would've put your foot down. You didn't!

This doesn't build respect and this is what makes people pleasing so tragic. In your mind, you think you're earning their respect because they like you and they can't get enough of your help. But in their mind, you have just become a tool. You've just become a means to an end.

And ultimately, you have no personality. Is that what you want for yourself?

3. You Lose Spending Precious Time With People Who Truly Matter

Let's get real here. If we were to reduce all the people in our lives to the ones that truly matter, if you do it right, you would end up with a handful of people. You don't end up with an army of people who are equally important and substantial. That's not reality.

At the end of the day, when it comes to your loved ones, you can count them with one hand or you should be able to count them with one hand even if you come from a large family. The ones who truly deserve to be called your "loved ones" are few and far between.

The problem with people pleasing is that everybody is equally important to you. You're so afraid of stepping on people's toes or disappointing people that ultimately, you can not tell who is truly important and worth loving from everybody else.

At the end of the day, you give up your life pleasing everyone and anyone only to end up alone, broken and rejected. How come? Your real loved ones also need your attention and they need a lot more of it than everybody else.

If you are spreading yourself too thin emotionally, you will not invest the proper amount of time and cultivation in those relationships. They would still love you, but at a fairly shallow level. It won't be as deep as it could otherwise have been. This is the great personal tragedy of people pleasing.

4. You Jeopardize Your Own Work

Everybody's got their own life's work. For most people, this involves raising a family. Our families are usually our legacy. We may not have been able to achieve much with our lives. We may have felt disappointed with certain hopes and dreams that we may have had. But at least we have a second generation.

When we look at our child, we can see our second chance. It's not unusual for parents to view their children as the extension of their ambitions, hopes and dreams. But a lot of people also have something bigger than just leaving a second generation. They want to build something. They want to have some sort of impact on their world.

But unfortunately, you can kiss all of that goodbye if you find yourself always giving priority to anybody and everybody else. You're not prioritizing your own. So you end up jeopardizing whatever legacy you are capable of producing.

Please understand that most people are inefficient. Don't be surprised if you're one of them. In the space of 8 hours of a typical work day, actual productive work can be boiled down to 1 hour or 2 hours if you're lucky.

If you spend all your productive hours doing somebody else's stuff, where does that leave your legacy? Here's the short answer. You end up nowhere.

5. Your Leadership Skills Suffer

There's a concept of servant leadership. It is Judeo Christian concept and it's very powerful and very relevant. But even in that context, when you serve, there is an overarching imperative. When you show kindness to other people, it's because you are shining a light to a larger group imperative that you yourself are commanding them to follow.

Well, the problem is when you are pleasing people, this service is misdirected. You're not serving other people to serve as some sort of example so people can then follow your lead. No! That's not happening. When you serve other people because you're a people pleaser, it is intended for their needs right there, right then.

It is very shallow and, ultimately, whatever benefits it brings to the table doesn't last long. This is not leadership. You may have a title in your company's organization chart, but it's useless because people will lose respect for you.

They don't see that you have some sort of overarching agenda and whatever service you do for others serves only to highlight that agenda. You're not bringing people home when you just bend over backwards randomly because you're afraid that they will talk behind your back.

6. You Become Wishy Washy

Whenever you're serving many people at once, it's hard to make a decision. It really is. Why? When you make a decision, somebody has to necessarily lose. Get over that fact. Accept it. It's high time you embrace it.

But the problem is if you're a people pleaser, you hang on to this fantasy that there is such a thing as an all encompassing "winning solution". This solution is good for everybody at all times and in all places. That's a fiction.

Decisions cut. Decisions hurt. Many people win. But some people have to lose. You're just going to have to accept that fact of life.

7. You Lose Yourself

The most ironic effect of people pleasing is the idea that you are actually putting yourself first by earning other people's respect or preserving their good will. They're not doing any of that. Seriously! People will start looking at you as some sort of "tool" or "go to solution".

They don't look at you as a person. They just look at you as a solution. This is especially true if you agree with them regardless of how disagreeable their opinions are.

8. People Pleasing Erodes Your Mental Health

When you constantly suppress your opinions and thoughts because you're afraid other people might disapprove of them, this can slowly make you crazy. You are entitled to your thoughts. You are entitled to your opinion because you're a human being.

All human beings on an individual level are entitled to this. When you find yourself internally censoring yourself or editing your thoughts, you are suppressing your humanity. You have the right to be heard. You have a right to your own opinion and you have a right to express it.

When you suppress all of this and hold it in, that pressure mounts. This can slowly corrode your mental health.

9. You Attract Abusive People

I hate to break this to you, but there are a lot of bad people out there. These are people who don't just cut corners or take advantage from time to time. These are people who actually get off making other people miserable.

Don't be surprised if you come across somebody who would make all sorts of demands for you not because they need those favors done. They just want you to go around in circles. They just want to feel that they have some sort of slave. They just want to get the satisfaction that they have some sort of hold over you.

I know, it sounds diabolic. But yes, those people do exist and sadly, you attract those kinds of people when you automatically try to please others. These people are sick. They love the fact that you care about their opinions so much that you would deny your own needs. That gets them off.

Chapter 3: How Becoming "Not Nice" Is Your Gateway to Rewarding Life

First, let me begin with the benefits of overcoming people pleasing and finish off with an overview of the 6 things that you need to do to overcome this problem.

What do you stand to gain?

What are the personal benefits of stopping people pleasing?

Benefit #1: You learn to be more assertive

By being more assertive, you learn to speak up for yourself and this is the healthiest thing you can do. You stand out. You can take pride in the fact that your opinion is being counted. Now, of course, rejection is part of the territory. So is opposition.

The moment you stand up, expect that there will be some people who will not like what you have to say. You can also expect that some people will put up a fight. Guess what? This is part of life!

Benefit #2: You will finally be able to set boundaries

When you set boundaries, you establish freedom. When you set boundaries, people start to respect you because they know that there is a line they can not cross. This makes you more likable, not less.

Benefit #3: You gain self confidence

When you stand up for what you believe in and you affirm your personal boundaries, you become more confident. How come? Setting boundaries is a form of personal competence. Research studies show that competence is the real fountain head of confidence, not self esteem.

Benefit #4: You earn real respect

This should be self explanatory. There's no respect gained when people know, at the back of their heads, that you are a doormat. However, they will respect you when they know that when they push to a certain degree, you will push back and then some.

They may not like it, but they at least will respect you.

Benefit #5: You are unlikely to bottle up resentments and anger

People pleasers are actually some of the most bitter and unhappy people. You can tell just by looking at them. They're smiling at you because they don't want you to feel offended or to think that there's something wrong with them.

But deep down inside, there's a tremendous amount of resentment and anger and guess what? Just like any volcano, anything hot, pressured and volatile kept locked down beneath the surface will eventually blow up.

Well, you let go of all of this! When you speak up and when you say no, it feels good. So instead of bottling this resentment and anger, it never materializes in the first place and you preserve your emotional health. How about that?

Benefit #6: You discourage manipulation, verbal attacks and emotional abuse

The worst kind of users are people who get what they want from others and then still stab them in the back. Believe me. You will run across those people if you are a people pleaser. It seems that no matter how you bend over and no matter how much you try to please them, it is not good enough.

They're angry, miserable and bitter and in their minds, why should other people not share their state of mind. When you say no, you draw a firewall against those people. They'll try to manipulate you, they'll talk behind your back, they might even conspire against you.

But guess what? People already know that they know all about them. You're not doing them any favors by giving in to them. You become part of the solution.

Benefit #7: You practice integrity

I hate to say it, but if you're a people pleaser, you're a liar. Seriously! You know who you are deep down inside. Deep down inside, you don't want to do this. You've got better things to do.

But since you're so afraid of this person talking behind your back, you end up doing it.

In other words, you don't live with integrity. You know the truth, so it's high time you live it out. When you learn how to say no and stop people pleasing, you start living a life of integrity.

Benefit #8: Inner peace

When you live a life of integrity, you get inner peace. You may not be the most popular person in the world, but it doesn't matter. You'd rather be in a state of peace and harmony because that's where your strength comes from.

If you have this inner strength, you will be able to help more people. Believe it or not, people pleasers, no matter how popular they may seem, are very weak and fragile inside. They have no real power. How come?

Their power depends on other people continuing to like them. And this trend will only continue if they continue to give in. Talk about weakness.

Benefit #9: You free up your time

When you cut out a lot of the unnecessary favors you're doing for other people, you free up a tremendous amount of time. You can then devote this time to the things that truly matter in your life.

This means cultivating your relationship with your loved ones. This can also mean cultivating your mind and becoming a better person. This can mean investing time in the gym and becoming healthier.

Whatever the case may be, you have more time for yourself.

Benefit #10: You achieve successful

Let me tell you, it's very hard to find really successful people who are people pleasers. In fact, I would be so bold as to say that it's impossible.

Truly successful people go out on a limb. They take risks. You can't do that when you're pleasing other people because somebody somehow, someway will feel offended. So you retreat. You feel small. You shrink. That's not a winning strategy.

THE PLAN TO OVERCOME PEOPLE PLEASING

Now that you have a good idea of what you stand to benefit from your decision to stop people pleasing, here are the 6 things you need to do to get away from people pleasing.

1. Be Authentic

This is the fountain head of overcoming people pleasing. You have to keep it real. To keep it real, you must first know who you are. Once you have a clear idea of who you are, who you want to be and what you stand for, stick to it. welcome to the world of authenticity.

2. Renew And Transform Your Mind

Whatever you choose to believe will dictate your reality. Beliefs are simply filters for reality. They help us interpret and make sense of the world around us. When you change this, you can stop being a people pleaser and start being a winner.

3. Set Up The Right Boundaries

Putting up healthy boundaries enables you to focus on your strengths while at the same time reminding you of your all too real limits. This also builds respect in the eyes of other people because they know they can't push up to a certain point.

As the old saying goes, good fences make for good neighbors. This saying also applies to invisible, aka psychological and social, fences.

4. Build Up Your Self Esteem

Self esteem is your estimation of your value as a person. In other words, you look at yourself and think if whether you're worthy and you come up with ideas regarding what kind of person you are. It's hard to develop a healthy self esteem when you're always afraid of what other people would think.

By saying no, you regain and you build up your self esteem.

5. Set Your Priorities

Once you have a clear idea of who you are, you would have a clear idea of your character. Once you have a good picture of the character you want for yourself, your values will kick in. Prioritize these.

6. Assert Yourself

Once you have followed the previous steps, then you have something to assert. You have something to stand on. You have something to fight for. When people see this, they give you respect and, ironically enough, admiration.

The most lovable people are not exactly the most agreeable people. There are many polarizing personalities throughout history and even in your life right now. But guess what? Many of the things that turn people off about certain personalities in your life are exactly the kinds of things that make others fall in love with them.

Life is ironic, no?

Chapter 4: Embrace Authenticity: Learn How To Say No Without Feeling Guilty

The foundation of any kind of assertiveness training is reality. If you can wrap your mind around who you really are, chances are you're going to have a tough time asserting yourself, if for anything, you don't know which part of you to assert.

Please understand that people have many different sides. There are people who we wish we could be, there are individuals and personalities whom we think people want us to be, and of course, there is who we really are. You have to have a clear idea as to who you really are.

Unfortunately, a lot of people make a big deal about "being real." They are clueless; they don't know their authentic selves. You have to make a decision: Who are you? This is very painful for a lot of people, because let's face it, when individuals look at themselves in the mirror, often times they do not like who they see.

The good news is you can choose to accept who you really are, warts and everything. You don't have to be perfect. You don't have to become somebody else. You just have to learn to accept who you are, and build on what you have. This is the first step in truly asserting yourself in many areas of your life.

Otherwise, you're like an actor trying to present "the real you" that you have absolutely no clue about. It is no surprise that people-pleasers get dumped on, used, abused, and manipulated precisely because they don't respect themselves enough to know themselves. A little bit of authenticity helps, but the bottom line here is you have to know who you are in the first place.

This is not as easy as you think. If you've been spending all these years trying to please people, trying to be all things to all people who may not necessarily care all that much about you, in many cases, you probably would find yourself shadowboxing.

Self-Respect

Being yourself means respect and acceptance. Again, you may not look all that good to yourself. Maybe there are a lot of things that you are embarrassed about. Maybe there are certain things you did in the past that you are ashamed of. But you have to accept those before you can move on.

There is a very common thread among people who are trying to achieve some level of visit involving selfishness. They think that they are being selfish, or self absorbed, if they try to reconnect with their real selves.

If you think about it, this is the best thing you can do for other people. You're doing them the favor. When you go around trying to please everybody, because you're hanging on to some sort of illusion of who you think you are, you're ultimately not doing anybody any favors.

You're definitely not doing yourself any favors. You're not respecting yourself, you're not giving yourself the kind of self-love you deserve.

In a July 2014 study, in the Journal of Counseling Psychology, 232 college students were surveyed regarding the connection between life satisfaction and a sense of authenticity. This was a pretty intensive study that tracked two time periods in the lives of these public university students.

The study showed that those who acted with a greater sense of authenticity at the first test or survey period, expressed higher life satisfaction and less stress when they were interviewed at the second time period. The bottom line is if you think you're being authentic, you're more likely to be happy.

The study suggests that a deeper sense of authenticity leads to a better sense of well-being. In a 2013 study, in the journal Psychological Science, 132 participants were randomly split up into two groups. They were asked to recall a situation in their lives, and describe it as either authentic or inauthentic.

The first group were asked about a situation where they felt authentic. This means that they were actually conducting themselves based on their values, personality, belief systems, and who they imagine themselves to be. They were then asked to relive that situation.

In the other group, people were asked to recall a time where they felt they were not being true to themselves. Basically, they were asked to imagine that situation, and how it felt. After both groups went through this process, they were asked to take a test that tried to gauge or measure their happiness level.

Remarkably, people who were instructed to focus on periods of authenticity in their lives were happier. If you want to be truly at peace with yourself, and you want to live a happier life, with less depression and anxiety, start with authenticity.

Step-by-Step Instructions for Boosting Authenticity

Follow the steps below to reconnect with your authentic self. Please understand that this is just a framework. Everybody is different, so feel free to tweak these and make them fit your personal circumstances.

Step #1: Know yourself

I know this is easy to say, but like I said, all of us have these heaps of identities that we made up for ourselves, or other people imposed on us. You have to zero in on what you think makes sense in your life. In other words, you're going to have to pick that particular self whom you think best lines up with values you yourself chose.

I'm not talking about the person your parents wish you were. I'm not talking about who other people think you are. I'm talking about who you want to be. Ultimately, identity is a choice.

Of course, there are biological limits to it. There are also social and cultural considerations, but ultimately, it all boils down to the power of the individual. So pick that identity.

Step #2: Pick apart the identity you have chosen

There's no such thing as a perfect identity. All of us have angels and demons; we're all sinners and saints. Accordingly, look at your strengths, but also take a long, hard look at your weaknesses.

What are the things that are holding you back from truly achieving great things with your life? What are your fears? What are the things that make you feel stubborn or prideful?

Step #3: Decide your ideal self

This is where your personal power comes in. You have a lot more power over your life than you give yourself credit for. Understand that people who achieve great things with their lives all started their journey with a decision. They decided to stop being the old person that they were, with the old results and failures, and decided to try something new.

Now, it's your turn. Pick the kind of values you'd like to pursue. Pick the kind of character you would like to possess. Please understand in none of these steps can you find the idea of reputation.

Forget about reputation. Because reputation is what people think they know about you. It's limited to what they can see. Focus more on what they can't see. Focus more on who you are behind closed doors. In other, zero in on the character you want to build for yourself.

Chapter 5: Change Your Mind Change Your World

What if I told you that reality is an illusion? What if I told you that you are the editor or writer of your reality? This is not crazy. This is backed up by science. If you want a stripped-down example of how this plays out, take the case of two guys walking down a street corner and seeing a beautiful Ferrari.

One guy looks at that piece of Italian automotive engineering and says, "There's no way I can afford that, I'm too poor. The rich get richer. Life is unfair. Life sucks." Now the next guy, looks at the exact same car, and thinks, "What do I need to do to buy a car like that? What do I need to change to get something like that?"

Now let me ask you, which of those guys have a higher chance of eventually ending up with a

Ferrari? Make no mistake, it's not the first guy. When you look at the statements that he said to himself, he basically sealed himself off from any possibility of victory. When you say to yourself, "I'm ugly, I'm dumb, I'm stupid, I'm depressed, I'm poor." You are judging yourself.

You are willing these realities into existence. You are speaking pain, mediocrity, limitation, obstacles into your life. Instead of judging yourself, why not ask questions? Did you know that you are a very resourceful and creative person? Did you know that you have a tremendous amount of imagination trapped within you?

If you ask yourself questions, you trigger these. You tap into these capabilities which then bubble to the surface in seemingly small forms, but if you choose to focus on them, they scale up over time, and they grow in power.

In other words, they achieve a sense of momentum that delivers more and more victories in your life. When you ask yourself "How can I live in a 10,000-square foot mansion?" You ask yourself, basically for a map.

Maybe you're working in a minimum-wage job right now. So how do you get from that point to where you want to go? That means you probably need to get promoted. You probably need to scale up your skills.

Once you find the courage to do that, then you're ready to level up; maybe you need to get a master's degree? Maybe you need to start your own business. You see how this works? It all boils down to our initial mindset. Mindset is everything.

In a study published in the journal Social Cognitive and Affective Neuroscience, in 2016, the idea of a "growth mindset" was associated with the ability to adapt one's behavior, and learn from one's mistakes.

In other words, there is a close connection between the ability of a person to try, fail, try again, fail, and keep trying until they succeed. This was kind of fuzzy at first, but ultimately, it boils down to how we choose to process stimuli.

Just because you face a defeat, doesn't mean it's the end. Just because you encounter a No, doesn't mean that all avenues are closed off to you. Mindset is everything. If you were a people-pleaser, your mindset is you cannot live without other people's validation. Your mindset is that you cannot survive without people supporting you.

Not surprisingly, you become addicted to their approval, and you become extremely fearful of their judgment and criticism. This is all a mindset choice. It's not set in stone. It's definitely not locked into your DNA.

In another study in the European Journal of Social Psychology, in October 2010, researchers probed into the question of how habits can be broken and formed. I discuss habits here because your mindset is a habit.

Please understand that stopping smoking, quitting sex addiction or drug addiction, they all flow from a mindset. And if you have the right mindset, it's easier to lose addictions and adopt the right habits.

For the longest time, there was an idea that it takes 21 days to adopt a habit or effect behavioral change. While it turns out according to this study of 96 volunteers, asked to adopt a healthier lifestyle involving their diet and exercise, that it takes 66 days. And a key part of this is the participants changing their mindset, or at least their perspective on the changes that they're doing.

In the same way, you're going to have to change your habit of constantly seeking other people's approval. Ultimately, they cannot live your life for you. Ultimately, no matter how much they respect you, and how much they like you. You're going to have to live your life.

There are many popular people who commit suicide. There are many people who have a lot of social esteem, but lack self-esteem. So focus more on what's important. Focus on your attitude towards yourself, which is locked into your mindset.

At the very least, adopt a mindset that asks the right questions, so you are empowered to do more and achieve more, instead of constantly judging yourself, and putting yourself in a neat, tidy little box and compartmentalizing yourself away from your fullest potential. You have a lot to offer, and unfortunately, when you have a judgmental mindset regarding who you are, what you're capable of, and what the "good life" is, you sell yourself short.

Please understand that you have to stop blaming other people for this. Maybe you had an abusive mother who told you that you wouldn't amount to much. Maybe you had a father that was emotionally absent and couldn't care less about what you are doing. Maybe you had a boyfriend, or a girlfriend who abused you.

You have to let that go, and understand that they've moved on; it's high time you did the same. Focus on what makes sense to you now. Focus on choosing your reality, and a key part of this is choosing the right mindset that would take you from point A to point B.

In other words, you go from a victim who is constantly addicted to people's approval, to a victor who produces his or her own reality on a take it or leave it basis. It's great if get approval, but you don't live or die by it. You have your own agenda. You have your own future to make. I hope you understand the difference. A key part of this is changing your mindset.

Chapter 6: Discover the Magic of Self Care

Self-care is a necessity. It is not a luxury. People-pleasers, like yourself, constantly put other people's needs ahead of yours. But just because that has become habitual, doesn't mean that you no longer need to be taken care of.

In fact, it has gotten so bad to a lot of people-pleasers, that they think that the moment they speak up about their needs, they're being selfish. They beat themselves up. They have internalized this martyr complex, because they have accepted and resigned themselves to being some sort of emotional doormat.

This really is sad, because if you cannot love yourself, don't expect other people to. The whole idea of meeting people that will "complete" you works in the movies, but nowhere else.

Self-care is an absolute necessity. It is not an option. It is not a luxury. It is definitely not something that "would be nice if it happened." You have to have it right here, right now.

But here's the secret: The only person that can give you the self-care you need is yourself. It should be obvious, but the problem is people who are addicted to others' approval are completely mystified by this. They believe that the more they make other people smile, the more they please other people, the more they become.

They're only playing games with themselves. As I have mentioned in the opening chapters of this book, the more favors you do for other people, the less you become in their eyes. It becomes so much easier for them to take you for granted. It becomes so much easier for you to become yet another face in the crowd. If you think you're feeling small now, wait until you repeat what you've been doing for several more years.

Any idea of self completely disappears because you have become so hopelessly addicted to what other people would think. Break the chain by making it a habit to take care of yourself first. This doesn't close off the possibility of you taking care of others. Don't get me wrong, you can still do that, but you have to assert priority. You have to take care of number one first.

This isn't being selfish, because when you take care of yourself psychologically, emotionally, physically, spiritually, you become more complete and more powerful. And this puts you in the position to not only help more people but help them better.

The problem is when we are so focused on living for other people and pleasing them, we neglect ourselves. We may not be all there mentally, emotionally, and spiritually. Try as hard as we might, we are not able to give us much as we thought we could.

This really is too bad because people-pleasers are likely to overindulge. They give and give and give, and then they end up with comfort-eating. They feel like garbage. They feel like something's missing. So what do they do? They raid the fridge. They do drugs. They find empty sexual relationships. This is all unhealthy, you know it, i know it, everybody around you knows it.

In a case Western Reserve University study, that came out in February 2012, in the Journal of Social and Clinical Psychology, researchers found that people-pleasers dealt with social pressures by eating.

In a two-stage study involving 101 College students, participants were filtered based on their tendency to put the needs of others before their own. They were asked whether they were worried about hurting other people, or were they watching their words because they are sensitive to being criticized, and other behaviors typical of people-pleasers.

Once their tendency for people-pleasing was identified, a female actor came in the same room. The actor was then offered by the researcher M&M candies. The actor would take a certain amount and then the bowl of candy was offered to the study participant.

Participants were then asked how many candies they took and why. It turns out that people with people-pleasing mindsets took more candy, because they want to please the female actor who took candy ahead of them.

This then leads to the inference that when there is more pressure, and food is part of the equation, people tend to eat more food. People pleasers deal with social stress by eating more food. This study highlights the need for an alternative.

If you're in a stressful social situation, and maybe somebody said something that cut you or make you feel lousy, your first instinct shouldn't be to eat, or smoke, or have sex with strangers, but maybe it should be something healthier like meditation, regular exercise, reading.

Practice Better Self-Care

Realize that it begins with you

The first thing that you need to do is stop looking for a knight in shining armor, or looking for people to change 180 degrees and start treating you better. You can't wait for somebody else to start giving you the care that you owe yourself.

The only way to do this is, of course, to lean on the authenticity that you built in chapter 4. Acknowledge your flaws and weaknesses; embrace them. You don't have to be perfect.

69

It's very important to understand that everybody screws up, everybody makes mistakes. Everybody has a past that can be filled with shame, embarrassment, and humiliation. But just because something bad happened, they don't have to necessarily define who you are, and limit where you could go.

Self-care begins with embracing your responsibility to do the best with what you have. In other words, you focus on how things are instead of how you wish they would be. This means giving yourself honor. This means drawing the limits around yourself.

Eating healthier, setting rules regarding your sleeping schedule, and making time for exercise, reading, meditation, mindfulness. This also means that you have to monitor your stress levels. In chapter 5, you learned to change your mindset.

Give yourself the opportunity to test that. Think about a stressful image; maybe it's the father who abandoned your family. Maybe it's the ex-girlfriend who screwed around behind your back. Maybe it's the best friend who stole from you.

Whatever the case may be, show that mental image in your mind, and allow yourself to separate any emotional judgment from the mental image. Keep repeating this in a relaxed environment. Eventually, you will reach a breakthrough.

You will think about things. You will remember things, and come across people, or hear certain stimuli that no longer throw you off track. It no longer makes you feel vindictive. It no longer makes you feel incomplete, broke, inadequate, or defective.

Instead, it feels like you have a deep core of assurance regarding who you are. And when these negative thoughts come, they flow slowly over your head like a cloud. They don't have to rain on you. You don't have to hang on to them, and you definitely don't have to let them define you.

It also helps if you read a lot. I'm a professional writer, so I'm pretty biased regarding this, but when I read literature, I step out of myself. I break free from my personal drama and I enter a new world.

And the most liberating part of this is I know it's fake. I know this is fantasy, so when I'm in a new world, I don't have to be somebody else. I don't have to let my past beat me up. I don't have to feel lousy.

I don't have to worry about stuff that's around the corner. Instead, I just look at the page, read the words, and find myself in a different place, feeling different things, and this is the most liberating thing in the world. Take a walk.

Now, a lot of people might think this is corny, but you'd be surprised as to what you can discover when you are mindfully walking around your block. I don't care where you live, maybe you live in a very crowded neighborhood, or maybe there's a lot of open space in your area. Just take a walk.

When you walk, your lining up your mental faculties with your spiritual dimension, as well as your physical body. This lines up, because when you pay attention to small details, like the leaves of a tree, or the way the sunlight hits a certain outdoor scene, you get an opportunity to reconnect with how you process reality.

Are you the type of person who constantly judges the things that you perceive? When you see somebody new, do you always relate them to somebody that hurt you or somebody that you're afraid of. Or do you just take things one at a time? Do you appreciate beauty as you find it in the present moment?

This is a very powerful skill to have, and unfortunately, it is a skill that you will only master and remember when you do it. You can think about all you want, but until and unless you actually live it out, it won't be real.

So take a daily walk. You'd be surprised how a small daily habitual walk can change you from the inside out.

Chapter 7: Learn To Set Boundaries You Can Stand By

You're reading this book because you have a tough time saying no to people. You'd bend over backwards trying to please people, and they step all over you again and again, you know it. Obviously, you are miserable enough to read this book.

The problem is people find it hard to say no, because they don't want to be rejected. They don't want people to think bad things about them. They don't want to be labeled as rude. They definitely don't want to hurt other people's feelings.

It all starts off with a sense of obligation, but it's a slippery slope. Sooner or later, you end up disrespecting yourself, because that's really what happens, because when you come across people, who get off on pushing and pushing and pushing until they feel that they completely own you, you're not doing that person any favors.

That person is warped. That person gets off on dominance. You, on the other hand, are broadcasting to other people around that it's perfectly okay to treat you like garbage. It's perfectly okay to take you for granted, and ultimately, to disrespect you.

The first step in breaking free out of this people-pleasing mindset and mental addiction is to remember the concept of limits.

Tap The Power Of Limits

Since you've been spending all this time trying to please others, and do favors for everyone, and waste your time doing so, you may be under the false impression that you have no limits. After all, you're doing all these flavors. After all, it seems like you have all this time. Well, think about the opportunity costs.

You can't be at two places at once. When you are living somebody else's life for them, you're not living your own. When you're doing one thing, you're not exploring something else, which may turn out to be much better for you in the long run.

You are basically going around in circles. You are chasing your tail. The key here is to realize that limits do exist. If anything, the whole idea of opportunity costs highlights the concept of limitations. It's a limitation in capability, it's a limitation in time, it's a limitation in utilization of your resources.

In other words, limits come out again and again. Now, I want you to embrace that idea. Instead of wishing it away, or thinking that somehow, some way it doesn't apply to you, embrace the idea of limits.

Go From Limits To Boundaries

Now that we are clear that limits do exist in your life, the next step is to use these practically by creating boundaries. This is where it gets tricky, because this is going to apply across the board.

You must establish boundaries at work, you must establish boundaries in your friendships, you must establish boundaries in your romantic relationships. You definitely have to establish boundaries when it comes to your family.

Boundaries, as the old saying goes, makes for great neighbors. When a neighbor builds a fence, they're literally drawing a line on the ground, basically saying, "This is where I begin and end. This is where you begin and end."

This limitation and understanding, which is obvious to everyone involved, is then the foundation for a relationship based on respect.

Because there is no mutual respect when your neighbor can safely say, "Well, my boundary is all the way to the front door of your house."

He obviously didn't pay for that land, but you let him push his boundaries anyway. That doesn't create respect for you in his mind. You're a pushover. So understand how boundaries work, and insist on them across the board.

This has to take place in your relationships, at work, and in every other social interaction you find yourself in. Monitoring boundaries is a little tricky in human relationships, because it's too easy to use technology, to encroach, manipulate or stalk.

In a 2011 survey study that appeared in the Computers of Human Behavior Journal, 804 undergraduate students were surveyed regarding how they use technology in their intimate relationships. It turns out that females were more likely to look into the email account of their partners.

Only 6% of males said that they would monitor their partner's emails. This study highlights the role technology plays in setting boundaries. In this case, females were more likely to violate boundaries using technology compared to their partner.

This also highlights the need for setting clear rules in relationships. Basically, things like browser histories, mobile app data records, mobile device access, and of course, email, are definitely key areas you can talk to your partner about. Because these speak directly to how much boundaries and, by extension, respect you have for each other in your relationship.

Boundaries also imply trust, and people who can't help themselves but check their partner's browsers and email, obviously are not showing trust. Please understand that when you set these boundaries regarding which devices and which apps are off-limits, you don't have to explain.

There is no need for you to justify why you should get what you should have had coming to you in the first place. Trust should be assumed. Respect should be assumed in a relationship.

Interestingly enough, when you put your foot down, you are more likely to be respected by your partner, and the boundaries between you will become more tightly defined. And this can have the effect of enriching your relationship.

In a second study that came out in the journal Personality and Social Psychology Bulletin of March 2014, study participants requested strangers to do acts that can be deemed unethical. These ranged from vandalizing a book from the library, or telling a white lie.

The study featured actors talking to study participant to do uncomfortable, unethical things. Participants were then asked to rate how comfortable they are, and also indicate if they thought that the actions requested of them were unethical.

The survey showed that when people have a tough time defining boundaries, the obvious way to define the boundary, of course, is to simply say no. This study showed that when people are uncomfortable with turning other people down, they don't say no. Instead, they use of phrases like "I don't" or "I can't."

When you say "I can't," you're not really setting a boundary. What you're doing is you're passing the buck. You're saying that some sort of external force or arrangement or factor is preventing you from otherwise giving in to the request.

The good news is when people say, "I don't," they're saying something stronger than no. Because when you say no, there can be a variety of reasons why you can't draw the boundary at that point. Maybe you just don't have the time, maybe you were ill-disposed. Maybe, you just don't have the resources.

But when you say, "I don't," you're basically claiming something about your identity. When somebody asks you to do something unethical like vandalizing a book, or playing a prank on somebody, the moment you say, "I don't" you are proclaiming something about your character. You're basically saying,"I don't do that kind of thing, that is not who I am. That kind of behavior is not something I do."

The key takeaway here is to stop using "I can't" or other soft tactical words to a flat-out no. This study also instructs that we shouldn't just no. Opt for something stronger, say, "I don't." Basically, you're saying, "That's not who I am."

The more you do this, the more powerful your boundaries become, and the more authentic you fee, and you also exercise the change in your mindset that enables you to deal with other people better.

Chapter 8: Boost Your Self-Esteem to Become More Assertive

Comedians make a big deal out of self-esteem. I really can't blame them, because self-esteem is one of those concepts that, on its face, can be a source of humor. If you're suffering from low self-esteem, it means you don't have a high estimation of yourself. You don't place enough value on yourself.

You think you're not worth all that much, especially if you compare yourself to other people. Make no mistake, being a people-pleaser means you have low self-esteem. That's the bottom line.

It doesn't matter how confident you otherwise feel. It doesn't matter how good you feel when other people pat you back and compliment you.

None of that takes away from the fact that you are a people-pleaser, and because of that, you have low self-esteem.

Somebody with a healthy self-regard, or who places the appropriate amount of worth on himself or herself, won't please other people. You won't bend over backwards putting yourself last, or sacrificing your interests on behalf of others.

You won't put all this time, effort, and resource going along just to get along, because ultimately, you know how to put your foot down. You know who you are. You know what's important. You give yourself enough respect because you think you are important enough.

Self-esteem really boils down to that fundamental question: How important do you think you are? Are you worthy or sacrificing for? Are you worthy of all this effort and investment? Are you worthy?

Your task in this step is actually very simple. Realize that people-pleasing is an indication of low self-esteem. Stop dancing around the issue. Stop trying to hypnotize yourself. Stop pretending that it's otherwise. Accept the truth: People-pleasing means you have low self-esteem.

The next logical question

Now that you have established that people-pleasing is a key indicator of low self-esteem, the next logical question to ask yourself then is, "What are you going to do about it?"

The best way to break out of the self-esteem trap is to re-orient your sources of value, or your measurement of value away from other people. You basically have to say to yourself "I am worthy because I am. Not because of what I do for other people, not because of the good things people say about me, not because of my reputation, not because of my family, I just am worthy."

Now, at first, this may ring hollow, but if you follow all the previous steps, eventually it will sink in. You just have to be as conscious about this question as much as possible. Don't dodge it. Don't sweep it under the rug. Don't pretend it doesn't exist. Keep at it, put it front and center. Dwell on it, meditate on it. It is worth your time and effort.

It may seem you're just rehashing a lot of psychological and emotional baggage, but ultimately, you're investing in setting your life right. You are realigning your mental furniture so you can live a life of power, significance, and true lasting impact.

Your self-esteem must come from you. That's the punch line of many comedians, because there is an inherent humor there. People talk about self-esteem, but ultimately, deep down inside, you know that they're talking about getting esteem from other people. How can that be? How can you get from others what you should be giving yourself?

Self-esteem is about choosing to be happy with what you have. It's about being optimistic about your prospects. It's about trusting yourself more. I can go on and on. The good news is if you follow the previous steps, everything will fall into place.

You would have a map in front of you. It won't be just this mysterious fog in front of you. You won't be shots in the dark. Instead, everything will become bright, clear, and well-defined because you lived out the steps I have walked you through in previous chapters.

Learn to take pride. There's nothing wrong with saying I am worthy. There's nothing wrong in being proud of your capabilities. There's nothing wrong with serving yourself first. There's nothing wrong with achieving things for yourself, because you want to, not because you're trying to impress other people, or because you're trying to live up to some sort of standard.

The only standard that matters, as far as your self-esteem and mental health go, is your standard. It has to make sense to you.

Affirmations work

Try self-affirmations that come to mind as you do the previous steps. These affirmations like "I'm good enough," "I can make things happen," or "I am powerful." It may seem shallow, but the more of your experiences tie into these statements, the stronger they become. They start infusing your present reality with a power you thought you did not have.

This is backed by science. In the April 2015 issue of the journal Personality and Social Psychology Bulletin, 134 participants were put through power relationship scenario. Similarly, in other experiments, negotiation, and personal persuasion skills were tested.

The bottom line is when people were given positions of power, they perform better under pressure. When they were told that they had a certain title, they felt more in control. The takeaway here is you have to give yourself that power. You have to give yourself that title. You have a lot more control over your mental and emotional state than you give yourself credit for.

Chapter 9: Practice Day To Day Assertiveness

In the previous chapters of this book, I've shared with you key scientific insights as well as practical day to day tips. It's now your turn to turn that information into lived reality. You have to act on these. You have to carry them out.

You can't just kick them around in your head as ideas that "would be nice" if they actually worked. This is not college. This is not university. This is definitely not high school. I'm not sharing this information with you so you can mentally file it away as some sort of academic learning.

This information can and will change your life if and only if you act on them. In other words, you have to assert yourself on a day to day basis.

Take The Opportunity To Assert Yourself

If you're completely honest with yourself, you would realize that you have a tremendous amount of opportunities to assert yourself every single day. If you find yourself in line and there are people cutting in line, that's an opportunity.

If you have gone to a Starbucks and the barista gave you the wrong drink or the drink wasn't made according to your personal preference, that's an opportunity. When a friend of yous says something that offended you or struck you as odd or a little bit off, that's an opportunity to speak up.

If you think about it hard enough, there are so many opportunities you could take to become a more assertive person. The reason why you may think that these opportunities are few and far between or are restricted to purely formal situations is because you have been a people pleaser for so long. That's the bottom line.

If you've been doing things a certain way, you start blocking things out. In fact, you assumed certain things simply don't exist because you're used to thinking a certain way.

Well, if you followed the previous steps, you have taken the blinds or torn down the scales from you eyes. You will be able to start seeing things for how they really are. Sure at first, it's not going to be a pretty picture. There are many things that you would realize that you would rather not deal with.

There are many things that are uncomfortable or inconvenient. But you have to learn to live in reality if you want to assert your power over it. This is your reality. Your life is your possession. Don't let anybody make you think otherwise. Don't let anybody convince you that you are somehow, someway, lacking control. No!

You edit your reality. Whatevers happening in your life is happening because you allowed it to happen. You always have a choice. This is very painful for a lot of people to listen to because ultimately, it boils down to responsibility. When you fully embrace the idea that everything in your life takes place because you either chose it or you allowed it to happen, then you know what happens next.

You have to pick and choose. You have to take responsibility. You have to stop blaming people. You have to stop making excuses. You have to stop walking on egg shells and constantly trying to overlook that 800 pound elephant in the room.

In other words, you have to quit all the normal shenanigans people play with themselves in order to avoid deep, profound and, often times, painful personal truths. But as the old saying goes, no pain, no gain.

When you're growing, there's always pain involved. When you grow from a 3 foot child to a 6 and a half foot adult, your bones would've stretched, your muscles would've broken down and healed themselves many times over, you can bet that there's a tremendous amount of pain in the picture.

But at the end of that process, you're a beautiful adult. You're fully grown. It doesn't matter whether you're 5 feet tall or 7 feet tall or any point in between. You are who you are. So don't be afraid to go through the discomfort or even outright pain of growing.

Learn to be assertive because all these opportunities are all over the place. Any time you are dealing with another person on a 1 to 1 basis, there is an opportunity to speak up. There will be that chance to say to that person, "Hey, this is what I feel. This is my opinion. This is the personal impact of what you said to me." In other words, there's that opportunity.

The More Opportunities You Take, The Easier It Becomes

I want you to think back to when you first learned how to ride a bike. Do you remember those painful times? If you were like most kids, that part of your life was very physically painful. I know it was for me.

I remember my dad buying this old bike and he told me and my brother to keep practicing on the bike. He purposely bought an old bike because he knew that we were going to beat it up and scuff and scratch it as we try to learn.

Sure enough, that's precisely what happened. Every time I put the bike up and I get on top of it to ride it, I would fall. The wheels would crash against the ground and I would scrape my knee.

This went on for several days until that moment of truth.

That's when things just made sense. Everything just fell into place and I was able to pedal again and again and go in a straight line. It didn't happen overnight. But when it happened in that flash, there was no turning back. That was the point of no return.

In other words, I have achieved my breakthrough moment. All of us are capable of this. I use this example because this applies to everything in your life. This definitely applies across the board. You're having a tough time being assertive.

Well, you will only reach that breakthrough moment when you take all the opportunities you can find. At your work place alone, there are a thousand and one opportunities to share your opinion, speak up for yourself, be part of the conversation and push back.

Don't think that you're being a jerk. Don't think that you're stepping on people. Don't think that you are taking something that you don't deserve when you speak up for yourself. If anything, you're just reclaiming what you own. You're just reclaiming what you should've had coming to you in the first place.

Does this mean people won't be shocked? Of course not! After all, you're turning over a new leaf. Maybe you're showing them a side of you that they have rarely seen before. Not only do you have to adjust, but they have to adjust too. And guess what? It's high time they did that.

Being a people pleaser may have defined you for so long. But it doesn't mean that there are no other parts to you. It doesn't mean that all people can see in you and expect from you is some sort of emotional doormat.

It doesn't have to play out like that. The only person that can turn things around is you. So take that opportunity. Tap the power of momentum. The good news is the more you do something, the better you get at it.

Why do we get better with repetition?

When you take one assertiveness opportunity after another, eventually, you'll get the hang of it. eventually, things will fall into place and will become easy. How does this work out? Why does this happen in the first place?

Well, it really all boils down to emotional intimidation. When I was learning how to ride a bike, I was emotionally intimidated. I know how bad it hurts when I fall from my bike. So this whole process of getting up on the bike and trying to pedal in a straight line was very painful. It really took it out of me.

But the good news was every time I got on the bike, pedaled and fell down, I learned something new. At the very least, I learned not to let the process scare the stuffing out of me. And before I knew it, I was able to get back on my bike the moment I scratched or cut my knee open.

My skin was all bloody, but it didn't bother me because I knew I had to get back on the bike. I did it over and over again until I achieved that moment of truth. I was able to achieve a breakthrough. The same applies to you.

I understand that at this point, the whole idea of taking opportunities for assertiveness is downright scary. I get that. But the moment you say goodbye to that fear is the moment you will start leaping forward to your breakthrough moment.

Instead of being scared about all these opportunities for you to assert yourself and push back, look at it as an adventure. Look at it as something that you can look forward to. Look at it as a grand adventure in which you explore different parts of yourself.

These are parts of yourself that you've been running away from. In fact in the case of many habitual people pleasers, these are parts of themselves that they thought never existed. So do yourself a big favor. Reconnect with that part of yourself. Be authentic. Get real. Be true to yourself.

When you do this habitually, people will respect you more. As I've mentioned in an earlier chapter in this book, good boundaries make for great relationships. Set your boundaries. Insist on them. Do it day after day, week after week, month after month, year after year. Before you know it, the quality of your life will improve across the board.

Conclusion

It would be a tragedy if you take the information I share with you on this book and mentally file it away like you would lessons you learned in Algebra class. After all, who in their daily lives use their Algebra skills?

For the information that I've shared with you in these chapters, to have a deep profound and lasting impact on your life, you have to do one simple thing: do them. Live them out.

Please understand that people pleasers must realize that the only thoughts and feelings that they can change are their own. It's hard enough trying to change yourself. Can you imagine trying to change other people?

It doesn't make sense for you to continue to blame other people for what's wrong in your life. It doesn't make sense for you to keep looking at the past, for whatever it is, that hurts you or limits you in the present.

It is your responsibility. Your life is your choice. Whatever it is that you are unhappy with, whatever it is that you are content with, whatever it is that you are struggling with, you have allowed it to happen or you have actively chosen that outcome.

No amount of denial, no amount of blame finding and no amount of excuses is going to make this reality go away. The sooner that you own up to this, the faster you will go on the road to becoming a fully assertive, fully autonomous and fully powerful person worthy of respect.

Please understand that the only approval you need is your own. The bottom line is regardless of how many times you bend over, regardless of how quickly you give in to other people's demands, there will be people you can not please. Not in a million years.

For whatever reason, they will always find something to criticize. They will always find something deficient in what you did. So stop playing this game where you feel that you will only have self esteem and you will only allow yourself to be happy if other people around you are happy 100% of the time.

The truth is you can't change what other people think. They're a product of their past. They're a product of their experiences. Let them be. Focus on that one person you have full and total control of. Focus on yourself.

You have to understand that the more energy, time and effort you invest in trying to win people over, the less time you have available to build yourself up. Find yourself and stay true to yourself. Build on that foundation and you'd be surprised what kind life you can build for yourself. I wish you nothing but happiness, success and peace.

DISCLAIMER

While all attempts have been made to verify the information provided in this publication, the author does not assume any responsibility for errors, omissions, or contrary interpretations of the subject matter herein.

potential source of further information does not mean that the author endorses the information the individual, organization to website may provide or recommendations they/it may make. Further, readers should be aware that Internet websites listed in this work might have changed or disappeared between when this work was written and when it is read.

Adherence to all applicable laws and regulations, including international, federal, state, and local governing professional licensing, business practices, advertising, and all other aspects of doing business in any jurisdiction in the world is the sole responsibility of the purchaser or reader.

Made in the USA
Columbia, SC
12 May 2019